COMPUTER HARDWARE AND TROUBLESHOOTING

PROF. SHILPA R. YADAV

Made with ♥ on the Notion Press Platform
www.notionpress.com

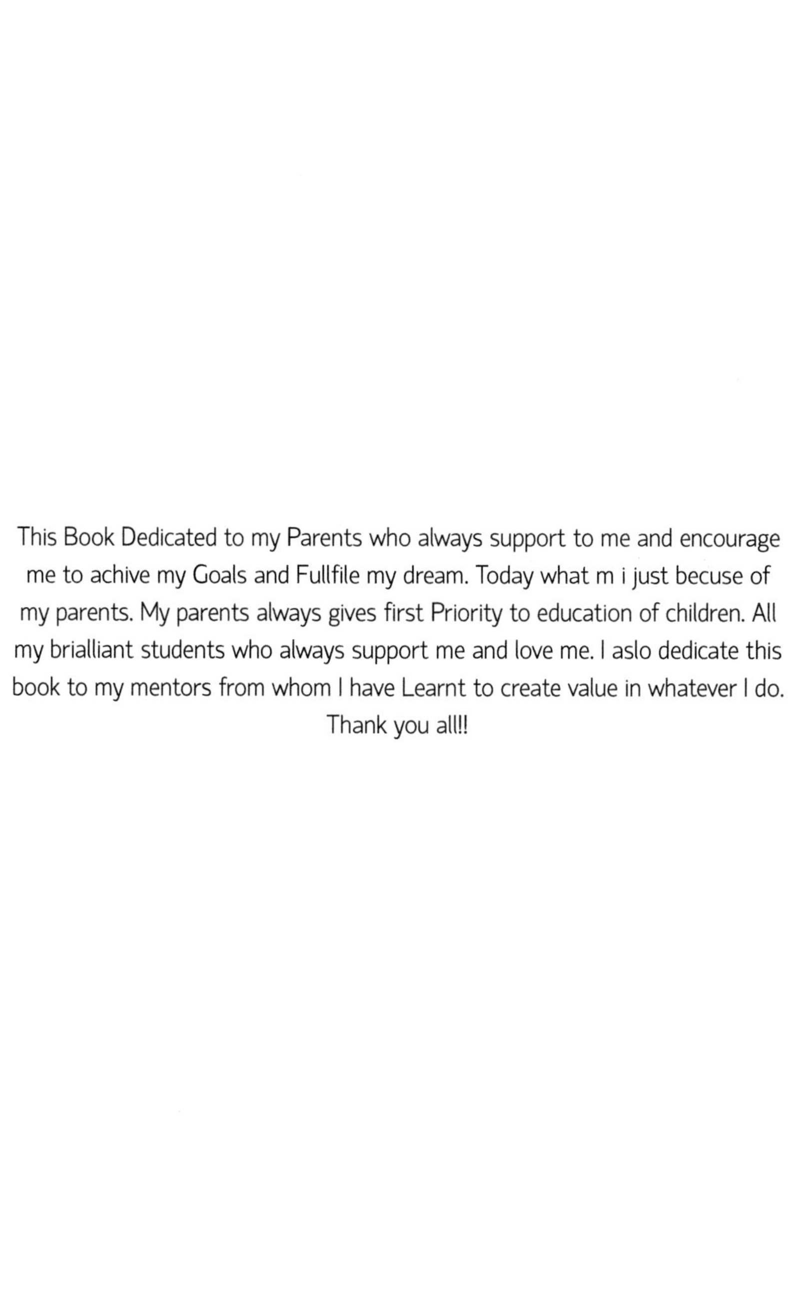

This Book Dedicated to my Parents who always support to me and encourage me to achive my Goals and Fullfile my dream. Today what m i just becuse of my parents. My parents always gives first Priority to education of children. All my brialliant students who always support me and love me. I aslo dedicate this book to my mentors from whom I have Learnt to create value in whatever I do. Thank you all!!

Contents

Acknowledgements

I am thankful to my parents today for their blessings and the constant support.

I want to thank EVERYONE who ever said anything positive to me or taught me something. I heard it all, and it meant something.

I special thanks to my mentors who always helped me and adviced me . I would like to thanks my husband Mr.Kamlesh Yadav who always appreciate me, believing in me and support me always to do best in career.

At the end, I want to thank God most of all, because without God I wouldn't be able to do any of this.

Prologue

The book covers the basics of computer hardwaree and allows the reader to gain experince in installing and configuring operationg system,loading and configuring drivers ,diagnosing errors and troubleshooting computer problems at both the components and software. The book intention of helping students develop the necessary abilities so they may achieve the following competency: Recognize faults, troubleshoot, repair, and perform preventive maintenance on computer systems and their peripherals.

CHAPTER ONE

Inside the PC: Core Component

What Is A Computer?

A computer is an electronic device that can accept data (input), alter data (process), and produce data under the control of instructions (software) stored in its own memory unit.Computers are electronic machines that can accept, process, and create information in response to instructions. A computer is a programmed electrical device capable of storing, retrieving, and processing data. A computer is a device that manipulates data in response to a set of instructions. The computer is an electronic device that accepts data as input, processes it according to instructions, and outputs the results.

Charles Babbage (1791-1871)
THE FATHER OF COMPUTER

A computer is an electro mechanical device which has capacity to accept ,store, process and retrieve data ,according to the user requirements.

In other words a computer is an electronic device that accept information(in the form of digitalized data) and manipulate it for some based on a program or sequence of instruction on how the data is to be processed.

1) Hardware: The term hardware refers to the physical components of a computer such as the system ,

- central processing unit,
- monitor, keyboard,
- computer data storage,

- graphic card, sound card and motherboard etc. A computer's hardware is comprised of many different parts, but perhaps the most important of these is the **motherboard.** The motherboard is made up of even more parts that power and control the computer.

2) Software: Software, commonly known as programs or apps, consists of all the instructions that tell the hardware how to perform a task. These instructions come from a software developer in the form that will be accepted by the *platform* (operating system + CPU) that they are based on. computer systems divide software systems into two major classes:

1. **System software:** Helps run the computer hardware and computer system itself. System software includes operating systems, device drivers and more. System software is almost always pre-installed on your computer.
2. **Application software:** Allows users to accomplish one or more tasks. It includes word processing, web browsing and almost any other task for which you might install software. (Some application software is pre-installed on most computer systems.

3) Firmware: Firmware is a very specific, low-level program for the hardware that allows it to accomplish some specific task. Firmware programs are (relatively) permanent, i.e., difficult or impossible to change.Firmware is part of devices (or device components) such as a video card, sound card, disk drive and even the motherboard. Firmware is data that is stored on a computer or other hardware device's read-only memory (ROM) that provides instruction on how that device should operate. Unlike normal software, **firmware** cannot be changed or deleted by an user .

GENERATION OF COMPUTER

1) First Generation: Vacuum Tubes (1940-1956)

2) Second Generation: Transistors (1956-1963)

3) Third Generation: Integrated Circuits (1964-1971)

4) Fourth Generation: Microprocessors (1971-1980)

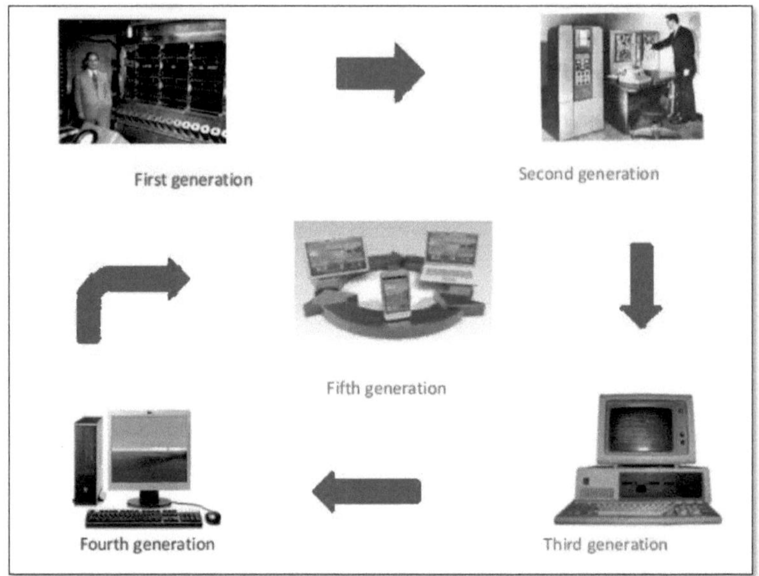

GENERATION OF COMPUTER

First Generation: Vacuum Tubes (1940-1956)

first generation computer,
vacuum tubes as CPU,
magnetic drum for data storage ,
and machines languages were used for giving instruction.

First Generation: Vacuum Tubes (1940-1956)

The computer of this generation was very large in size called room-sized computers. The programming of first generation computers was done in machine languages (0s and 1s). Afterward, assembly languages were developed and used in first generation computer.

These tubes, like electric bulbs, produced a lot of heat and the installations used to fuse frequently. Therefore, they were very expensive and only large organizations were able to afford it. The first generation computers used vacuum tubes as the basic components because vacuum tubes are the only electronic components available on those days. Vacuum tubes are used for circuitry and magnetic drums are used for memory.

The input to the computer was given through punched cards and paper tapes. The output displayed as printouts. No translator (translates from programming language to machine or computer language) was used to compile the programming language. The instructions to computer was given directly in machine language, i.e 0's and 1's. The first generation computers are mainly used for scientific research.

Features of first generation computers:

1)Technology used: vacuum tube

2)Machines languages were used to instruct the computer.

3)Magnetic core memory was used as primary memory.

4)Electrostatic tubes, paper tape, punch card, magnetic tape

5)Punched card, printing devices were used for input/output operations and store the result.

6)It occupies very large space, slow processing, inefficient and unreliable due to low accuracy.

7)Power consumption was very high and it generated much heat.

8)It could only perform straight forward simple numerical calculation.

9)Computer used to be much expensive.

Advantages

These are the fastest calculating computers at that time.

They perform operations in milliseconds.

Disadvantages

These computers are large in size.

Large amount of heat is emitted.

The cost is high.

These computers are non-portable.

The first generation computers solve only one problem at a time.

Air conditioning is required

Machine language is difficult to learn.

Second Generation: Transistors (1956-1963)

Second generation computers used Transistors magnetic tapes, magnetic disks for secondary memory and magnetic core for primary memory. **Second Generation**: Transistors (1956-1963) The world would see transistors replace vacuum tubes in the **second generation of computers**. The second generation computers used transistors as the basic components. The transistors were highly reliable and easier to handle and maintain than the vacuum tubes. They required much less power.

Second Generation: Transistors (1956-1963)

The transistor made the second generation computers faster, smaller, cheaper, more energy-efficient and more reliable than their first-generation computers. Second generation computers used the low level language i.e. machine level language and assembly language which made the programmers easier to specify the instructions.

The used small, long lasting transistor also increased speed and reliability. Internal processing speed increased. Vacuum tubes replaced by transistors as main logic elements. Magnetic taps and disk began to replace punched card as external storage device. The size of transistor is small compared to the size of vacuum tubes. Transistors are made from silicon.

Transistor

Features of second generation computers:

1) Use of transistors

2) Reliable in comparison to first generation computers

3) Smaller size as compared to first generation computers

4) Generated less heat as compared to first generation computers

5) Consumed less electricity as compared to first generation computers

Advantages

Perform operations in microsecond.

The size of second generation computers is small compared to the size of first generation computers.

The cost is low.

Maintenance cost of second generation computers is low because hardware failures are rare.

Disadvantages

Air conditioning is required.

Only used for specific purposes

Constant maintenance was required

The cost is high.

Punch cards were used for input.

Third Generation: Integrated Circuits(1964-1971)

The computers of third generation used Integrated Circuits (ICs) in place of transistors. A single IC has many transistors, resistors, and capacitors along with the associated circuit .

This development made computers smaller in size, reliable, and efficient. In this generation remote processing, time-sharing, multiprogramming operating system were used. High-level languages (FORTRAN, COBOL, PASCAL etc.) were used during this generation.

The electronic circuit formed by constructing electronic components like transistor, resistor and capacitor on a small piece of semiconducting material is called integrated circuit. Integrated circuit is also called as chip or microchip. Large number of transistors is placed on a single chip.

Third Generation: Integrated Circuits(1964-1971)

In third generation computers input is given through keyboard and output is displayed on monitor. The keyboard and monitor were interfaced through the operating system.

Operating system allows different applications to run at the same time. The instructions to the computer were written in high level language instead of machine language and assembly language. Instead of punched cards and printouts, users interacted with third generation computers through keyboards and monitors and interfaced with an operating system, which allowed the device to run many different applications at one time with a central program that monitored the memory.

Features of third generation computers:

1) IC used

2) More reliable in comparison to previous two generations

3) Smaller size

4) Generated less heat

5) Faster

6) Lesser maintenance

7) Costly

Advantages

The size of third generation computers is less compared to the size of previous first and second generation computers.

Generates less heat than the previous generation computers.

It can perform calculations in nanoseconds.

Maintenance cost is low compared to the previous generation computers.

Consumes less power than the first and second generation computers.

Disadvantages

Air conditioning was required.

Highly sophisticated technology required for the manufacturing of IC chips.

Fourth Generation : Microprocessors (1971-1980)

The fourth generation computers used LSI (Large Scale Integration) and VLSI (Very Large Scale Integration) technology. Using LSI and VLSI technology thousands of transistors are integrated on a small silicon chip. In fourth generation computers the semiconductor memory is replaced by magnetic core memory resulting in fast random access to memory.

VLSI circuits having and other circuit elements with their associated circuits on about 5000 transistors single chip made it possible to have microcomputers of fourth generation.

Fourth Generation : Microprocessors (1971-1980)

Fourth generation computers became more powerful, compact, reliable, and affordable. In this generation, time sharing, real time networks, distributed operating system were used. All the high-level languages like C, C++, DBASE etc., were used in this generation. Personal computer operating systems were developed during this period. It is not only increased the number of components but also improve their power ,efficiency and reliability.

Features of fourth generation computers:

1) VLSI technology used
2) Very cheap
3) Portable and reliable
4) Small size
5) Pipeline processing
6) No AC required
7) Concept of internet was introduced
8) Great developments in the fields of networks
9) Computers became easily available

Advantages

More powerful and reliable than previous generations.

Small in size

Fan for heat discharging and thus to keep cold.

No air conditioning required.

Totally general purpose

Less need of repair.

All types of High level languages can be used in this type of computers

Disadvantages

The latest technology is required for manufacturing of Microprocessors.

Classification of computer

1)Personal computer(micro computer)

2)Mainframe computer

3) Minicomputer

4) Super computer

Personal computer(micro computer)

A **personal computer** is a computer small and low cost, which is intended for personal use (or for use by a small group of individuals). Personal Computer (PC) consists of a CPU contains the arithmetic, logic, and control circuit on an single (IC) integrated circuit;

Personal computer(micro computer)

Two types of memory, main memory, such as RAM, and ROM, magnetic hard disks (HDD) and compact discs and various input/ output devices, including a display screen, keyboard and mouse, modem, and printer. The term micro-computer is generally synonymous with personal computer (PC), or a computer that depends on a microprocessor. Micro-computers are designed to be used by individuals. There are two sub categories in it. One is PC which is less in price & reliability, other is Workstation which is expensive in price & reliability comparing with PC Application : - Personal computer, Multi user system, offices.

Mainframe computer

A mainframe computer is a large ,powerful computer that handles the processing for many users simultaneously . They are larger and have more processing power than some other classes of computers minicomputers, servers workstations , and personal computers.

Mainframe computer has **processing units(PUs), memory, I/O channels, control-units** and **peripheral devices**. A **processing unit(PU)** is the **brain** of the mainframe computer, that executes instructions. A mainframe computer has many processors. They are used in large organizations where thousands of clients have to access data simultaneously.

Mainframe computer

Mainframe computers are those computers that offer faster processing and grater storage area. It is also known as Father computer.

Minicomputer

A minicomputer is multi-user computer that is less powerful than mainframe. These system are more powerful than micro computer and are also more expensive. It is a midsize computer. minicomputer is a multiprocessing system capable of supporting from up to 200 users simultaneously.

A minicomputer is a type of computer that possesses most of the features and capabilities of a large computer but is smaller in physical size. A minicomputer may also be called a mid-range computer. These are also small general purpose system. They are generally more powerful and most useful as compared to micro computer.

Super Computer

Super computer are those computer which are designed for scientific job like whether forecasting and artificial intelligence etc. They are fastest and expensive. A super computer contains a number of CPU which operate in parallel to make it faster.

The fastest type of computer Supercomputers are very expensive and are employed for specialized application that require immense amounts of mathematical calculations. For example, weather forecasting requires a supercomputer. Other uses of supercomputers include animated graphics , nuclear energy research, and petroleum exploration.

Motherboard

The most important part of a PC is the motherboard. It holds: the processor chip, memory chips, chips that handle input/output (I/O) , the expansion slots for connecting peripherals.

Some chips are soldered onto the motherboard(permanent), and some are removable (so they can be upgraded). A motherboard is one of the most essential parts of a computer system. It holds together many of the components of a computer, including the central processing unit (CPU), memory and connectors for input and output devices.

A motherboard provides the electrical connections by which the other components of the system communicate.it also contains the central processing unit and hosts other sub systems and devices.Motherboard is a large flat circuit board. It is covered with sockets, & other electronic parts .The I/O connectors are soldered on Motherboard. It consists of chips. Chips consist of transistors. It is also called System board, Planner board, Main board & also Mobo. It is a large flat multi-layered PCB (Printed Circuit Board) covered with sockets, other electronic parts and various chips.

A motherboard provides the electrical connections by which the other components of the system communicate. it also contains the central processing unit and hosts other sub systems and devices. Every piece of hardware directly or indirectly plugs into the motherboard.

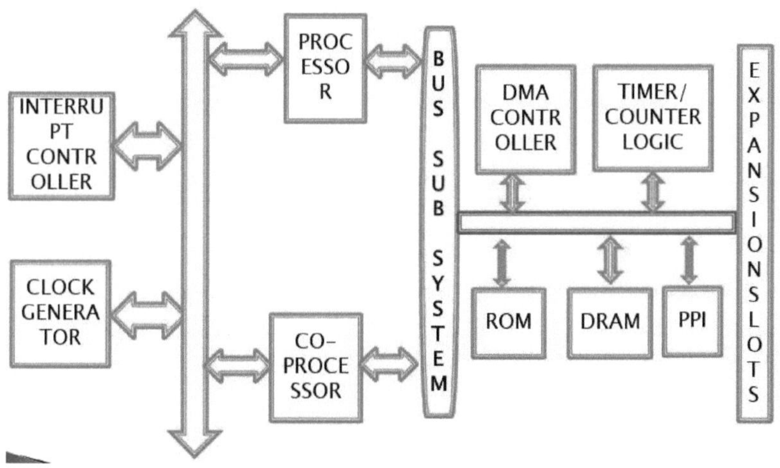

FUNCTIONAL BLOCK DIAGRAM:MOTHERBOARD

1) PROCESSOR :A processor is an integrated electronic circuit that performs the calculations that run a computer. A processor performs arithmetical, logical, input/output (I/O) and other basic instructions that are passed from an operating system (OS). The four primary functions of a processor are fetch, decode, execute and writeback.

The basic elements of a processor: The arithmetic logic unit (ALU), which carries out arithmetic and logic operations on the operands in instructions. The floating point unit (FPU), also known as a math coprocessor or numeric coprocessor, a specialized coprocessor that manipulates numbers more quickly than the basic microprocessor circuitry can. Registers, Which hold instruction and other data , supply the operands to the ALU and the results of operation.

The processor has two main sections.

1) Bus interface unit(BIU) :- The BIU can transfer the data between the microprocessor and other circuit.

2)Execution unit(EU) :- That carries out the instruction.

2) CO-PROCESSOR : A coprocessor is a special set of circuits in a microprocessor chip that is designed to manipulate numbers or perform some other specialized function more quickly than the basic microprocessor circuits could perform the same task.

The coprocessor, also known as a math coprocessor, numeric coprocessor, or floating-point unit (FPU), became a physical part of the microprocessor chip.

3) Clock Generator : A **clock generator** is a circuit that produces a timing signal (known as a clock signal).A clock generator is a type of circuit that produces a continuous, synchronized electrical signal for timing purposes in a wide variety of devices.

4) Bus sub system : Computer bus transfer data between components of computer system . A system bus is a single computer bus for the data transfer between the central processing unit and the memory.

5) Interrupt controller : The interrupt controller has 8 input lines that take requests from one of 8 different devices. The controller then passes the request on to the processor, telling it which device issued the request.

1)Mask able interrupt

2)Non-mask able interrupt

6) Direct memory access controller(DMA) : To speed up the system performance the main processor is to be relived from time consuming jobs like moving blocks of memory (bulk data)between main memory and I/O devices. DMA can also be used for “memory to memory “copying or moving of data within memory.

7) Timer /Counter logic : There are three timers on motherboard. Timer 0: Used to maintained the system time and date. Timer 1: Used to generates DMA request singles for performing refresh cycle at every 15 microseconds. Timer 2: Used to generates various tones by the speaker.

8) Peripheral Interface Logic(PPI) : The programable peripheral interface device connects the peripheral devices to the computer.

9) Expansion slots : An expansion slot is a socket on the motherboard that is used to insert an expansion card or circuit board, which provides additional features to a computer such as video, sound, advanced graphics, Ethernet or memory.

Chipsets : A **chipset** is a set of electronic components in an integrated circuit known as a "Data Flow Management System" That manages the dataflow between the processor , memory and peripherals. it controls communications between the processor and external devices, the chipset plays a important role in determining system performance.

Two types of Chipsets :

Northbridge Chipset: The Northbridge chipset on motherboard helps the CPU to work with RAM and Graphic card. The northbridge links the CPU to very high-speed devices, especially RAM and graphics controller, and the southbridge connects to lower-speed peripheral buses.

Southbridge Chipset : It handles mass storage devices, USB, PCI Bus and other expansion buses. The southbridge contains some on-chip integrated peripherals, such as Ethernet,USB, and audio devices.

RAM(Random Access Memory) : Random Access Memory (RAM). RAM is used to hold programs while they are being executed, and data while it is being processed. RAM is volatile, meaning that information written to RAM will disappear when the computer is turned off.

ROM(Read-Only Memory) : Read-Only Memory can be read but not changed. It is non-volatile storage: it remembers its contents even when the power is turned off. ROM chips are used to store the instructions a computer needs during start-up, called firmware.

Some kinds of ROM are PROM, EPROM, EEPROM, and CD-ROM.

CMOS Memory : CMOS stand : Complimentary Metal Oxide Semiconductor Random Access Memory (CMOS RAM). CMOS memory is the time and date, which is updated by a Real Time Clock (RTC). CMOS devices require very little power to operate. Memory chip located on the motherboard that stores the BIOS settings. Battery must be replaced when it becomes weak or you may lose the stored BIOS settings. Receives power from the battery that is installed on the motherboard. Clear the BIOS settings stored in the CMOS using the jumpers located on the motherboard or by removing the battery from the motherboard .

Cache Memory : Cache memory is a small-sized type of computer memory that provides high-speed data access to a processor and stores frequently used computer programs, applications and data. It is the fastest memory in a computer, and is typically integrated onto the motherboard and directly embedded in the processor or main random access memory (RAM).

Cache memory provides faster data storage and access by storing instances of programs and data accessed by the processor. when a processor requests data that already has an instance in the cache memory, it does not need to go to the main memory or the hard disk to fetch the data.

CENTRAL PROCESSING UNIT : The central processing unit (CPU) is the unit which performs most of the processing inside a computer. The **central processing unit (CPU)** of a computer is a piece of hardware that carries out the instructions of a computer program. It performs the basic arithmetical, logical, and input/ output operations of a computer system. The CPU has three components:

1) Control Unit: extracts instructions from memory and decodes and executes them.

2) Arithmetic Logic Unit (ALU): handles arithmetic and logical operations.

3) Memory unit:Control unit gets instruction from memory.

The CPU is the heart and brain of a computer. It receives data input, executes instructions, and processes information. It communicates with input/output (I/O) devices, which send and receive data to and from the CPU. The CPU has an internal bus for communication with the internal cache memory, called the backside bus. The main bus for data transfer to and from the CPU, memory, chipset, and AGP socket is called the front-side bus.

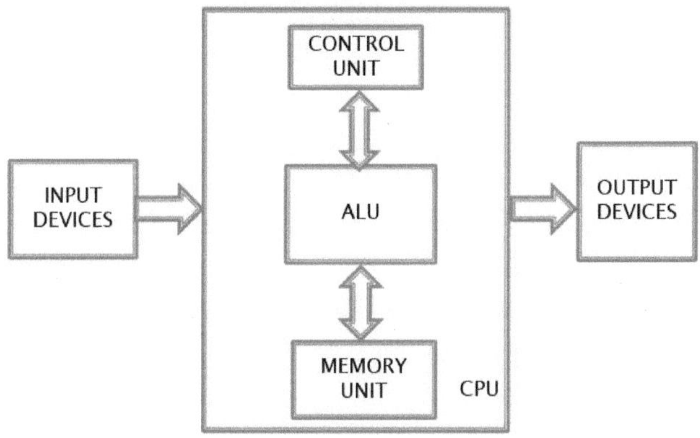

BLOCK DIAGRAM CENTRAL PROCESSING UNIT

Working : CPU consists of three basic units: control unit , Arithmetic Logical Unit (ALU) , memory unit Input is given through the input devices to CPU. Control unit controls communication within ALU and memory unit. Decides which circuit is to be activated. For reading instruction it uses Fetch-execute mechanism. Control unit gets instruction from memory. Control unit decides what to do of that instruction and transfers it to the ALU.

ALU performs various arithmetic operations like addition, subtraction, multiplication, division and logical operations like AND, OR, NOT, NAND etc. on that instruction. Results of ALU are stored in the memory or resistor for its further operations. After completing the instruction, stored results are passed to the output devices.

CPU performs four basic steps:

Fetch: Each instruction is stored in memory and has its own address. The processor takes this address number from the program counter, which is responsible for tracking which instructions the CPU should execute next.

Decode: All programs to be executed are translated to into Assembly instructions. Assembly code must be decoded into binary instructions, which are understandable to your CPU. This step is called decoding.

Execute : While executing instructions the CPU can do one of three things: Do calculations with its ALU, move data from one memory location to another, or jump to a different address.

Store: The CPU must give feedback after executing an instruction and the output data is written to the memory.

RISC (Reduced Instruction Set Computer) : That utilizes small and highly optimized set of instructions is termed as the Reduced Instruction Set Computer or simply called as RISC. It is also called as LOAD/STORE architecture. RISC by reducing the number of instructions required for processing computations faster than the CISC. The RISC architecture is faster and the chips required for the manufacture of RISC architecture is also less expensive compared to the CISC architecture. Pipelining technique of RISC, executes multiple parts or stages of instructions simultaneously such that every instruction on the CPU is optimized. Hence, the RISC processors have Clock per Instruction of one cycle, and this is called as One Cycle Execution.

CISC (Complex Instruction Set Computer) : The main intend of the CISC processor architecture is to complete task by using less number of assembly lines. For this purpose, the processor is built to execute a series of operations. Complex instruction is also termed as MULT, which operates memory bank of a computer directly without making the compiler to perform storing and loading functions. CISC have more number of predefined instructions which makes high level languages easy to design and implement.

CISC consists of less number of registers and more number of addressing modes, generally 5 to 20. CISC processor takes varying cycle time for execution of instructions – multi-clock cycles. Because of the complex instruction set of the CISC, the pipelining technique is very difficult. CISC consists of more number of instructions, generally from 100 to 250.

BIOS(BASIC INPUT/OUTPUT SYSTEM) : It also manages data flow between the computer's operating syetm and attached devices such as the hard disk , video adapter,keyboard,mouse and printer. BIOS controls input and output system. The BIOS stores the date, the time, and your system configuration information in a battery-powered, non-volatile memory chip, called a CMOS (Complementary Metal Oxide Semiconductor) after its manufacturing process.

A basic input/output system (BIOS) is a preinstalled program used during startup on Windows-based computers. The CPU initially accesses the BIOS, after which the operating system is loaded. A basic input/output system is also known as system BIOS or ROM BIOS. The primary purpose of the BIOS is to set up hardware and further load and start an operating system.

The BIOS checks every hardware connection and locates the devices, after which the operating system is loaded into computer memory. BIOS instructs the computer on how to perform a number of basic functions such as booting and keyboard control. BIOS is also used to identify and configure the hardware in a computer such as the hard drive, floppy drivc, optical drive, CPU, memory, etc.

four main functions of a PC BIOS :

POST - Test the computer hardware and make sure no errors exist before loading the operating system. Additional information on the POST can be found on our POST and Beep Codes page.

Bootstrap Loader - Locate the operating system. If a capable operating system is located, the BIOS will pass control to it.

BIOS drivers - Low-level drivers that give the computer basic operational control over your computer's hardware.

BIOS or CMOS Setup - Configuration program that allows you to configure hardware settings including system settings such as computer passwords, time, and date.

System Memory : The system memory is the place where the computer holds current programs and data that are in use. There are various levels of computer memory, including ROM, RAM, cache, page and graphics, each with specific objectives for system operation. memory is used in many different forms around modern PC systems, it can be divided into two essential types: RAM and ROM. ROM, or Read Only Memory, is relatively small, but essential to how a computer works.

CHAPTER TWO

Hard Disk Drive and Controller

Storage Device : A storage device is any computing hardware that is used for storing, porting and extracting data files and objects. It can hold and store information both temporarily and permanently, and can be internal or external to a computer, server or any similar computing device. A storage device may also be known as a storage medium or storage media.

Storage devices are one of the core components of any computing device. They store virtually all the data and applications on a computer, except hardware firmware. They are available in different form factors depending on the type of underlying device. For example, a standard computer has multiple storage devices including RAM, cache, and hard disk, as well as possibly having optical disk drives and externally connected USB drives.

There are two different types of storage devices:

Primary storage devices: Generally smaller in size, these are designed to hold data temporarily and are internal to the computer. They have the fastest data access speed, and include RAM and cache memory. Primary storage is also known as main storage, main memory or internal memory

Secondary storage devices: These usually have large storage capacity, and they store data permanently. They can be either internal or external to the computer, and they include the hard disk, optical disk drive and USB storage device. A secondary storage device is also known as an auxiliary storage device or external storage.

HARD DISK DRIVE (HDD) : A hard disk drive (HDD) is a non-volatile computer storage device containing magnetic disks or platters rotating at high speeds. It is a secondary storage device used to store data permanently, random access memory (RAM) being the primary memory device. Non-volatile means data is retained when the computer is turned off. All computers have a hard drive installed in them, which is used to store files for the operating system, software programs, and a user's personal files.

A hard drive can be used to store any data, including pictures, music, videos, text documents, and any files created or downloaded. Also, hard drives store files for the operating system and software programs that run on the computer. A hard disk drive (HDD) is a data storage device used for storing and retrieving digital information using rapidly rotating disks (platters) coated with magnetic material. An HDD retains its data even when powered off. Data is read in a random-access manner, meaning individual blocks of data can be stored or retrieved in any order rather than sequentially.

Main components for Hard disk drive

- Disk platter
- Stepper motor
- Spindle motor
- Read and write head
- Arm

DISK PLATTER : The platter is made up of a magnetic material, in the flat disk part of the drive. The data stored in the platter. Each set of magnetic particles is collection a unit called a bit.

STEPPER MOTOR : Use stepper motors for controlling read/ write head position. Stepper motors usually use +12V power, but some new low power drives use +5V power source.

SPINDLE MOTOR : It control the platter. It's motor rotates at a speed of 3600 to 10,000 r.p.m. All the platter moves in the same direction.

READ AND WRITE HEAD : The heads read and write the information to the drive platter. The head writes magnetic information on the platter.

HEAD ARM : Used for read and write operations. Read/Write head Is used for read/write data in magnetic Form.

HARD DISK INTERFACES:

1)SCSI **(Small Computer Systems Interface)**

2)IDE **(Integrated Drive Electronics)**

3)Serial ATA**(Serial Advanced Technology Attachment or SATA)**

4)EIDE**(Enhanced or Extended IDE)**

5)USB**(Universal Serial Bus)**

6)IEEE 1394 **(Firewire)**

7)SSD**(Solid State Drive)**

SCSI (Small Computer Systems Interface) : SCSI protocol defines how the devices communicate with each other via the SCSI bus. It specifies how the devices reserve the SCSI bus and in which format data is transferred. SCSI is a standard for parallel interfaces that transfers information at a rate of 8-bits per second and faster, which is faster than the average parallel interface. SCSI is the most popular interface for connecting high speed disk drives to higher performance PC's, such as workstations or network servers.

Small Computer Systems Interface

The SCSI controller (host adapter) functions as the gateway between the SCSI bus and the PC bus. The SCSI bus does not talk directly with devices, such as hard drives; instead, it talks to the controller that is built in to the drive. SCSI interfaces provide for data transmission rates (up to 80 megabytes per second). You can attach multiple devices to single SCSI port. SCSI drives are not too difficult to configure, but they are more complicated than IDE drives.

IDE(Integrated Drive Electronics) : IDE (Integrated Drive Electronics) is a standard electronic interface used between a computer motherboard's data paths or bus and the computer's disk storage devices. IDE is also known as Advanced Technology Attachment (ATA) or Intelligent Drive electronics (IDE). The IDE interface contains two IDE device connections and two motherboard connectors for two data cables. Advanced Technology Attachment (ATA) is a standard physical interface for connecting storage devices within a computer. ATA allows hard disks and CD-ROMs to be internally connected to the motherboard and perform basic input/output functions.

The ATA interface is basically a set of thin wires merged within a cable bus that are used to transfer data in and out of the disk drives. ATA supported parallel communication and was also called Parallel ATA (PATA).It consisted of a 40-pin controller cable and data transfer speed of 16-32 bits at a time. PATA was replaced by Serial ATA (SATA) - which has faster data I/O speeds. IDE drive can be directly connected to the I/O bus slot on the motherboard. Using 40 pin wire cable the IDE drive is connect to the bus adapter on motherboard.

Serial ATA(Serial Advanced Technology Attachment or SATA) : Serial ATA (Serial Advanced Technology Attachment or SATA) is a standard for connecting and transferring data from hard disk drives to computer systems. As its name implies, SATA is based on serial signaling technology, unlike Integrated Drive Electronics hard drives that use parallel signaling. SATA cables are thinner, more flexible and less massive than the ribbon cables required for conventional PATA hard drives. Serial ATA hard drives connect to a computer's motherboard via SATA controller hardware that manages the flow of data.

The SATA transport layer differs from PATA drives, in which data bits are delivered simultaneously across a 40-pin-wide ribbon cable. A Serial ATA drive transfers data in serial fashion. Data is moved one bit at a time between a SATA drive and its host, using a seven-pin data cable and 15-pin power cable. The SATA cable results in a higher signaling rate, which corresponds to faster throughput of data. SATA cables can be considerably longer than PATA ribbon cables, allowing a system designer more latitude in the physical layout of a system. The Serial ATA [SATA] bus is defined over two separate connectors, one connector for the data lines and one for the power lines.

EIDE(Enhanced or Extended IDE) : Enhanced integrated drive electronics (EIDE) is the hard drive interface that succeeded integrated device electronics (IDE), also known as ATA or ATA-1. EIDE is an improved version of the IDE drive interface that provides faster data transfer rates than the original standard. IDE drive controllers supported transfer rates of 8.3 Mbps, EIDE can transfer data up to 16.6 Mbps, which is twice as fast. The interface acts as an intermediary between the computer and a mass storage device. EIDE provides much faster transfer rates than IDE. EIDE is sometimes called fast ATA or fast IDE or ATA-2.

USB(Universal Serial Bus) : A Universal Serial Bus (USB) is a common interface that enables communication between devices and a host controller such as a personal computer (PC). It connects peripheral devices such as digital cameras, mice, keyboards, printers, scanners, media devices, external hard drives and flash drives. USB, Universal Serial Bus is one of the most common interfaces for connecting a variety of peripherals to computers and providing relatively local and small levels of data transfer. USB interfaces are found on everything from personal computers and laptops, to peripheral devices, mobile phones, cameras, flash memory sticks, back up hard-drives and very many other devices.

IEEE 1394 (Firewire) : IEEE1394 or **'firewire'** is a high speed serial bus. FireWire is a method of **transferring information** between **digital devices**, especially **audio and video equipment.** IEEE 1394, High Performance Serial Bus, is an electronics standard for connecting devices to your personal computer. It includes a plug-and-socket connection with a serial bus interface. Up to 63 devices may be connected at the same time with high data transfer speeds.

SSD(Solid State Drive) : SSD is an PC storage device that uses Solid State memory to store information. A solid- state drive also known as a solid state disk or electronic disk . It is a data storage device using integrated circuit assemblies as memory to store data persistently. SSD uses non volatile NAND Flash Memory , which enables it to retain data when the power is removed. A solid-state drive (SSD) is a data storage device that uses solid-state memory to store persistent data. SSDs use NAND-based flash memory or DRAM to store data.

Disk performance Characteristics:

Seeks Time : Seek time is the time taken for a hard disk controller to locate a specific piece of stored data.When anything is read or written to a disc drive, the read/write head of the disc needs to move to the right position. The actual physical positioning of the read/write head of the disc is called seeking. The amount of time that it takes the read/write head of the disc to to move from on part of the disk to another is called the seek time. Seek time is also measured in two other ways - track to track and full stroke.

Latency : Latency is a networking term to describe the total time it takes a data packet to travel from one node to another. when a data packet is transmitted and returned back to its source, the total time for the round trip is known as latency. Latency refers to time interval or delay when a system component is waiting for another system component to do something. This duration of time is called latency.

Data Transfer Rate : A data transfer rate (DTR) refers to the speed at which a device or network component can send and receive data. The data transfer rate of a drive covers both the internal rate (moving data between the disk surface and the controller on the drive) and the external rate (moving data between the controller on the drive and the host system).Data transfer is usually measured in bits per second. data transfer was sometimes measured in characters or blocks (of a certain size) per second.

HDC Functions : A hard disk controller (HDC) is an electrical component within a computer hard disk that enables the processor or CPU to access, read, write, delete and modify data to and from the hard disk.A hard disk controller's primary function is to translate the instructions received from the computer into something that can be understood by the hard disk. It consists of an expansion board and its related circuitry, which is usually attached directly to the backside of the hard disk.

The instructions from a computer flow through the hard disk adapter, into the hard disk interface and then onto the HDC, which sends commands to the hard disk for performing that particular operation. The type and functions of a hard disk controller depend on the type of interface being used by the computer to access the hard disk. For example, an IDE hard disk controller is used for IDE interface based hard disks.

Blu-ray disk specification : Blu-ray (BD) is a next-generation optical disc format. The format was developed to enable recording, rewriting and playback of high-definition video (HD), as well as storing large amounts of data. Blu-ray Disc (also known as BD or Blu-ray) is an optical disc storage medium designed to replace the standard DVD format. Its main uses are for storing High Definition Video, video games, and other Data storage applications. The name Blu-ray Disc derives from the Blue – violet laser used to read the disc.

****

CHAPTER THREE

Input Devices and Printers

WHAT IS AN INPUT DEVICE?WHAT IS AN INPUT DEVICE?

An input device is a hardware or peripheral device used to send data to a computer. An input device allows users to communicate and feed instructions and data to computers for processing, display, storage and/or transmission.

Because input devices are geared toward user-computer interaction, they are used to transform user actions or commands into electronic signals that are understood by computers. Any machine that feeds data into a computer is called an Input Device. Any device that interacts to any system and allows you to enter the information on the computer. An input device is a hardware or peripheral device used to send data to a computer. An input device allows users to communicate and feed instructions and data to computers for processing, display, storage and/or transmission.

KEYBOARD : External input device used to type data into some sort of computer system whether it be a mobile device, a personal computer, or another electronic machine. A keyboard usually includes alphabetic, numerical, and common symbols used in everyday transcription. Keyboard is the most commonly used input devices. They allow data entry into a computer system by pressing a set of keys neatly mounted on a keyboard.

Most keyboards have keys arranged in four groups:

Alphanumeric Keys : The alphanumeric keypad contains the alphabet and numbers as well as special keys such as Pause, Break and Print Screen.

Numeric Keypad : The cursor keypad (arrow keys) allow you to move the cursor between letters, words, sentences and paragraphs. The other keys (Home, End, Page Up, Page Down) allow your cursor to jump across larger sections and across screens.

Function Keys : A **numeric keypad** is the small, palm-sized, seventeen key section of a computer keyboard on the very far right.

Cursor-movement Keys : Keys that act as shortcuts for performing certain functions such as saving files or printing data.

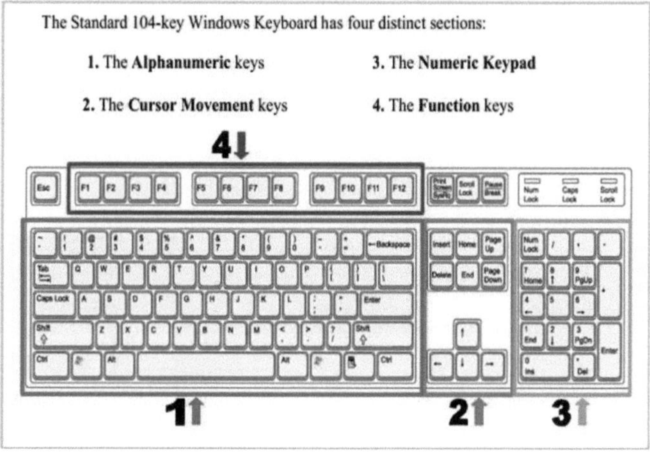

Types of keyboard :

Standard keyboard

Multimedia keyboard

Wireless keyboard

Components of keyboard : Mainly two component

1) Chip (microcontroller) :- Used to interface a keyboard with computer. It is main controlling device of keyboard. It reads signal coming from the keyboard matrix and interprets them . It has its own primary memory like ROM for storing program, we can also reprogram ROM

2) Key matrix :- Matrix of rows and columns. The switches are fabricated on these matrices in such a way that when we press a specific key , a specific row and column got short circuited and this will let the keyboard controller know that which key is being pressed.

Keyboard Working Principle : When you press a key: The keyboard controller detects the keystroke. The controller places a scan code in the keyboard buffer, indicating which key was pressed. The keyboard sends the computer an interrupt request, telling the CPU to accept the keystroke.

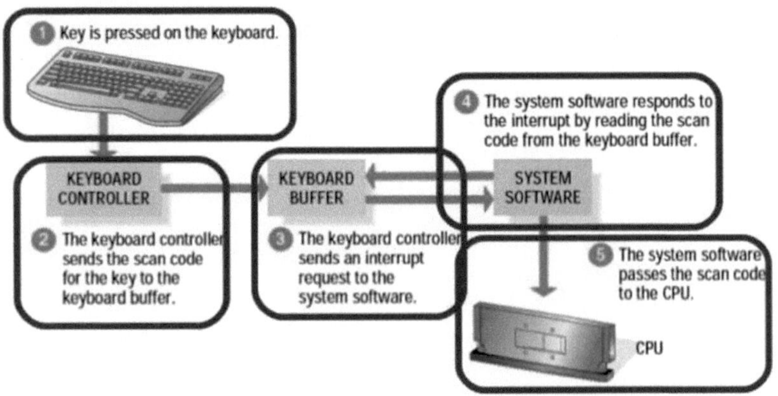

Keyboard interface : Keyboard interface is dedicated socket or connecter in computer for connecting a keyboard.

Two types of interface

1) Wired interfaces

A.DIN interface

B.PS/2 type interface

C.USB interface

2) Wireless interfaces

A.Bluetooth interface

B.Infrared interface

C.Radio frequency interface

Mouse : A mouse is a device that controls the movement of the cursor on computer screen. Some mouse have got two button while others will have a third scroll button in between the two. The plural of the mouse is mice.

Types of mouse

Mechanical :- Type of computer mouse that has a rubber or metal ball on its underside and it can roll in every direction. There are sensors within the mouse which are mechanical, detect the direction in which the ball is moving and moves the pointer on the screen in the same direction. A mouse pad should be used under the mouse to run on.

Optical :- This type uses a laser for detecting the mouse's movement. The optical mouse responds more quickly and precisely than mechanical and opto- mechanical mouse.

Opto-mechanical :- Same as mechanical mouse, but uses optical sensors to detect motion of ball. The device is a combination of optical and mechanical technologies, where the ball is present but the mouse movement is detected optically leading to more accuracy.

Laser mouse :- The laser mouse is new generation mouse with two necessary components . Light emitter Light detector. The laser mouse uses laser as light emitter and has a precise scanning of mouse movement.

SCANNER : A scanner is an electronic device that scan printed or handwritten text document, image, or particular object to convert them into a digital file format.

Types of scanner :

1.Flatbed scanner :- It is made up of glass pane and a moving sensor. The pane is illuminated with the help of bright light planted below it.The sensor and source of light move across the glass pane to scan the document and produce its digital copy. It scan up to A4 paper size. The item to be scanned does not need to be flate.

Flatbed scanner

2.Sheet fed scanner :- In it the document that is to be scanned is fed into the horizontal or vertical slot provided in the scanner. This scanner are most often used to scan single page document. It cant be used to scan thicker object like books, which is its major drawback.

Sheet fed scanner

3.Handheld scanner :- It is small manual scanning device which is moved over the paper that need to be scanned. In handheld scanner the hand needs to be steady all the time. Slight movement of the hand can lead to distortion of image. One of the most utilized handheld scanner is the barcode scanner . Typically used in shopping stores to valuate goods. The key advantage of the handheld scanner is portability. Drawback of handheld scanner is the limited area that can be scanned at the one time.

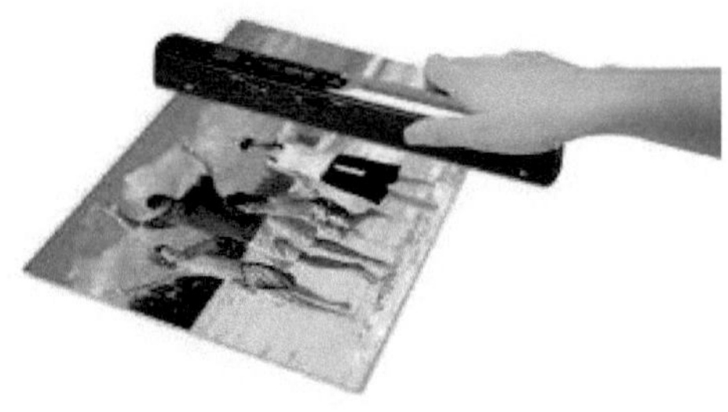

Handheld scanner

4.Drum scanner :- This type of scanner is rare because it is expensive compared to the other types of scanner . It gives higher resolution and color depth. Ideal for image that have to be enlarged . It is slow and require a high level of operator skill.

Drum scanner

5.Microfilm scanner :- Microfilm scanner are highly specialized devices for digitizing roll film and aperture cards(punch card). Getting good, consistent quality from a microfilm scanner can be difficult. Because they can be operationally complex. Only few companies make this and hence it has high cost.

6.Slide scanner :- Used to make digital copies of photos that you have stored as slide. Inserting each slide into the scanner and then pressing a button the result is that was previously only on a physical slide is now in digital form.

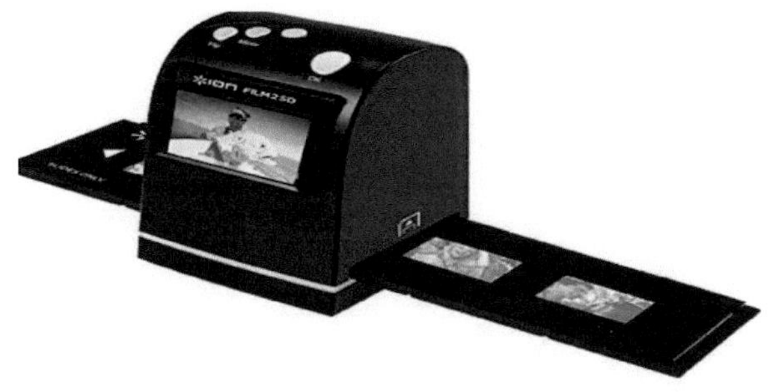

Slide scanner

PRINTER : A printer is electronic device which convert the text and graphical document from electrical form to the physical form. An external hardware device responsible for taking computer data and generating a hard copy of that data. Printers are one of the most commonly used peripherals and they print text and still images on the paper. A printer is a device that accepts text and graphic output from a computer and transfers the information to paper, usually to standard size sheets of paper. Printers vary in size, speed, sophistication, and cost.

The four printer qualities of most interest to most users are :

Color: Color is important for users who need to print pages for presentations or maps and other pages where color is part of the information.

Resolution: Printer resolution (the sharpness of text and images on paper) is usually measured in dots per inch (dpi). Most inexpensive printers provide sufficient resolution for most purposes at 600 dpi.

Speed: If you do much printing, the speed of the printer becomes important. Inexpensive printers print only about 3 to 6 sheets per minute. Color printing is slower. More expensive printers are much faster.

Printers can be divided into two main categories :

1) Impact printer

Daisy Wheel Printer
Dot-Matrix Printer
2) **Non-impact printer**
Ink-jet Printer
Thermal Printer
Laser Printer

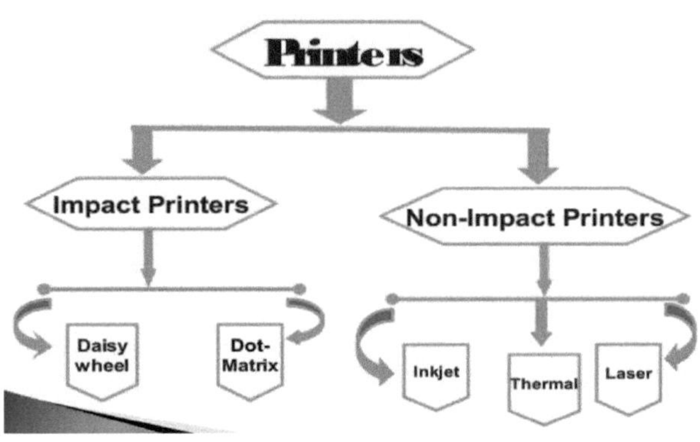

Classisfication of Printer

Daisy Wheel Printer :

A **daisy wheel printer** is an early type of impact printer invented in 1969 by David S. Lee at Diablo Data Systems. The printer uses a metal or plastic disk containing each of the letters, numbers, and other characters it supports. Daisy wheel printers were popular in the 1970s and 1980s, but are no longer used because of they have a low quality of print, are very slow, loud, and laser printers have come down in cost.

A daisy wheel printer is basically an impact printer consisting of a wheel and attached extensions on which metal characters are mounted. A daisy wheel printer produces letter quality print and it can't produce graphics output.In a daisy wheel printer, a hammer presses the wheel against a ribbon which in turn makes an ink stain on the paper in the form of a character mounted on the wheel extensions.These printers are very noisy as there occur great movement during the printing. Its printing speed is also very slow , less than 90cps(character per second).

Dot-Matrix Printer :

The dot matrix refers to the process of using dots to form an image. In a dot matrix image, the quality is determined by the number of dots per inch.Dot matrix printers use print heads to shoot ink or strike an ink ribbon to place hundreds to thousands of little dots to form text and images. Dot matrix printer uses a print head that runs back and forth, or in an up and down motion, on the page and prints by striking an ink-soaked cloth ribbon against the paper, like a typewriter.

Dot-matrix technology uses a series or matrix of pins to create printed dots arranged to form characters on a piece of paper.Because the printing involves mechanical pressure, these printers can create carbon copies and carbonless copies.This printer arranges dots to form characters and all kinds of images. The portion of the printer containing the pins is called the print head. The Dot Matrix printer, generally prints one line of text at a time. There are two approaches to achieve this: serial dot matrix and line dot matrix printer.

Ink-jet Printer :

Inkjet technology was developed in the 1960s, but first commercialized by IBM in 1976. Ink-jet printer is type of non-impact printer. It creates output on paper by spraying tiny drops of liquid ink. Inkjet printer has print-head that can spray very fine drops of ink. It consists of print cartridge filled with liquid ink and has small nozzles in form of m.It is a non-impact printer producing a high quality print. A standard Inkjet printer has a resolution of 300dpi. Newer models have further improved dpi.

An **inkjet printer** is a type of computer printer that creates a digital image by propelling droplets of ink onto paper. Inkjet printers are the most commonly used type of printer and range from small inexpensive consumer models to very large professional machines that can cost up to thousands of dollars.

How Inkjet Printer works?

1.Print head having four ink cartridges moves .

2.Software instructs where to apply dots of ink, which color and what quantity to use.

3. Electrical pulses are sent to the resistors behind each nozzle.

4.Vapor bubbles of ink are formed by resistors and the ink is forced to the paper through nozzles.

5. A matrix of dots called print head forms characters and pictures

Thermal Printer :

Thermal printers are inexpensive printers mostly used in fax machines. The Thermal printers are further classified into two types.

(1) Electro thermal printers

(2) Thermal Wax printers

A thermal printer is a printer that makes use of heat in order to produce the image on paper. Due to quality of print, speed, and technological advances it has become increasingly popular and is mostly used in airline, banking, entertainment, retail, grocery, and healthcare industries. Thermal printing does not make use of ink or toner unlike many other printing forms but largely depends on thermal papers for producing the images.They are also quiet popular in creating labels owing to speed of printing.

Laser Printer :

Laser printers use very advanced technology and produce a high quality output. Laser printers can also produce high quality graphics images.**Laser Printer** is a type of printer that utilizes a laser beam to produce an image on a drum.The light of the laser alters the electrical charge on the drum wherever it hits.The drum is then rolled through a reservoir of toner, which is picked up by the charged portions of the drumFinally, the toner is transferred to the paper through a combination of heat and pressure.laser printers are sometimes called page printers.In Laser printing, a computer sends data to the printer. Printer translates this data into printable image data. 5 pages can be generated in a single minute by using this method of printing.

General Troubleshooting :

1. Most printers, such as ink-jet printers, use a series of beeps to alert you or display a message that tell you a problem has occurred.
2. Paper jams are the most common type of printer problem. Most printers have panels that can be opened to check the paper jam.
3. Be careful when pulling a jammed paper, some printers contain many small sensors that may be damaged by forceful pulling.
4. To improve the quality of printed images, check the printer's documentation to find the size, composition and weight of the paper the printer can use.
5. You should clean your printer on a regular basis. You can use a computer vacuum cleaner or a can of compressed air to remove dust and dirt from most printers.

****

CHAPTER FOUR

Monitor and display adapter

Display unit is made up of two main parts

1.Video adapter

2.Monitor

The **video adapter** is a device that interface with computer and monitor . The **monitor** that display the text or graphics .

What is video?

It is a sequence of still images representing scenes in motion. Properties of video.

Video format basics

Video format are described by the following characteristics.

1.Standard

2.Image dimensions and aspect ratio

3.Frame rate

4. Scanning method

Video compression :

Video compression is the process of encoding a video file in such a way that it consumes less space than the original file and is easier to transmit over the network/Internet.It is a type of compression technique that reduces the size of video file formats by eliminating redundant and non-functional data from the original video file.

Usually video compression is done by removing repetitive images, sounds and/or scenes from a video. For example, a video may have the same background, image or sound played several times or the data displayed/attached with video file is not that important. Video compression will remove all such data to reduce the video file size.

Monitor : **VGA(video graphic array)**

VGA is popular display standard developed by IBM and introduced in 1987. it provide 640*480 resolution color display screen with refresh rate of 60Hz and 16 color display at a time. many revision of the standard have been introduced. The most common is super VGA (SVGA) , which allows the resolution greater than 640*480 such as 800*600 or 1024*768. a standard VGA connection has 15 pins and its shape like a trapezoid.

Monitor type :

1.**Digital monitor:** The older monitor which uses MDA, CGA and EGA video standard are called digital monitor. the data describing pixel color are sent from the video adapter to the monitor in a series of digital signal . for video card that can display only few color the digital monitor is preferable and also economical because the circuit is simple than analog. monochrome CGA standard and EGA standard monitors are common digital monitor.

2. Analog monitor : The analog type monitor use the VGA standard. It allows the transfer of color information from the video adapter to the monitor as analog signal.analog monitor support 256 different color values for each red, green , and blue color which make total of 16.7 million different color combination.

3. Multi scanning monitor : They can be suited with analog or digital video adapter. They can switch automatically or manual. Between analog and digital monitor.they contain more sophisticated electronics circuit which gives more flexibility to work on different display standard.

CATHODE RAY TUBE :

Stands for "Cathode Ray Tube." CRT is the technology used in traditional computer monitors and televisions. The image on a CRT display is created by firing electrons from the back of the tube to phosphors located towards the front of the display. Once the electrons hit the phosphors, they light up and are projected on the screen. The color you see on the screen is produced by a blend of red, blue, and green light, often referred to as RGB.

Construction:

1.An electron Gun : for producing a stream of electron.

2.Focusing band accelerating anodes: for producing narrow and sharply focused beam of electron.

3.Horizontal and vertical deflecting plates: for moving beam horizontally and vertically for controlling the path.

4.Screen: a glass envelope having phosphor coated screen which produce bright spot when struck by high velocity electron beam.

Working :

1.To produce an image, the beam is turned on or off.

2.The video information from the computer is used for turning the beam on or off at appropriate places when the beam scans the screen.

3.An electron gun at one end emits an electron beam

4.This beam is directed toward the screen.

5.When beam strike on screen, the phosphor coating on the screen produces illumination at that spot

6.The electron beam deflected horizontally and vertically using horizontal and vertical plate .

Digital Display Technology

1.Thin Displays

2.Liquid Crystal Displays

3.Plasma Displays

4.Light Emitting Displays

Liquid Crystal Displays :

Stands for "Liquid Crystal Display." LCD is a flat panel display technology commonly used in TVs and computer monitors. Like light-emitting diode (LED) and gas-plasma technologies, LCDs allow displays to be much thinner than cathode ray tube (CRT) technology.It is also used in screens for mobile devices, such as laptops, tablets, and smartphones.An LCD is made with either a passive matrix or an active matrix display grid. It is combination of two states of matter, the solid and the liquid.

Modern LCDs typically use active-matrix technology, which contain thin film transistors, or TFTs. These transistors include capacitors that enable individual pixels to "actively" retain their charge. Therefore, active-matrix LCDs are more efficient and appear more responsive than passive-matrix displays.

Plasma Displays :

A **plasma display** is a computer video **display** in which each pixel on the screen is illuminated by a tiny bit of **plasma** or charged gas, somewhat like a tiny neon light. **Plasma displays** are thinner than cathode ray tube (CRT) **displays** and brighter than liquid crystal **displays** (LCD).It is commonly used in large TV displays of 30 inches and higher. Plasma displays are also known as gas-plasma displays.

Two plates of glass are taken between which millions of tiny cells containing gases like xenon and neon are filled. Electrodes are also placed inside the glass plates in such a way that they are positioned in front and behind each cell. The rear glass plate has with it the address electrodes in such a position that they sit behind the cells. The front glass plate has with it the transparent display electrodes, which are surrounded on all sides by a magnesium oxide layer and also a dielectric material. They are kept in front of the cell.

Light Emitting Displays :

LED Display (light-emitting diode display) is a screen display technology that uses a panel of LEDs as the light source. Currently, a large number of electronic devices, both small and large, use LED display as a screen and as an interaction medium between the user and the system. Modern electronic devices such as mobile phones, TVs, tablets, computer monitors, laptops screens, etc., use a LED display to display their output.A light-emitting diode (LED) is a device that emits light when an electric current passes through it.

Light Emitting Diodes (LEDs) are the most widely used semiconductor diodes among all the different types of semiconductor diodes available today. Light emitting diodes emit either visible light or invisible infrared light when forward biased. The LEDs which emit invisible infrared light are used for remote controls.A light Emitting Diode (LED) is an optical semiconductor device that emits light when voltage is applied. In other words, LED is an optical semiconductor device that converts electrical energy into light energy.

Thin Displays/Thin film display :

A display screen made with TFT (thin-film transistor) technology is a liquid crystal display (LCD), common in notebook and laptop computers, that has a transistor for each pixel .Having a transistor at each pixel means that the current that triggers pixel illumination can be smaller and therefore can be switched on and off more quickly. TFT is also known as active matrix display technology . A TFT or active matrix display is more responsive to change. For example, when you move your mouse across the screen, a TFT display is fast enough to reflect the movement of the mouse cursor.

Graphics card :

A graphics card is a type of display adapter or video card installed within most computing devices to display graphical data with high clarity, color, definition and overall appearance.A graphics card is also known as a graphics adapter, graphics controller, graphics accelerator card or graphics board.The video card is intermediate chip between your monitor and CPU.The main job of video card is take the data which produce by the processor and translate them into the form that can be understand by computer monitor.Video adapter do all the computing task which was earlier did by CPU.

Video chipset: it does the calculating function. It sometimes referred as video coprocessor or accelerator.

Video BIOS: it provide a set of video related function that are used by programs to access the video hardware.

Video RAM: CPU store image detail in video RAM.

RAMDAC: in order to display image on screen the information in video RAM must be converted to analog signal and send to the monitor and this is done by the RAMDAC.

****

CHAPTER FIVE

Trouble Shooting and Preventive Maintenance

POST (Power-On Self-Test) :

Stands for "Power On Self Test." POST (or P.O.S.T.) is a series of system checks run by computers and other electronic devices when they are turned on. On computer systems, the POST operation runs at the beginning of the boot sequence.If all the tests pass, the rest of the startup process continues automatically. PCs run a POST each time the computer is booted up or restarted.

When the problem is identified with the system during the POST, the BIOS will use three methods to represent the problem.

1.**Beep code:-** Beeping pattern on the speaker.

ex: five beep means , processor may fail.

2.**Error code:-** for every error there is specific code which describe nature of error.

ex: error code from 100 to 199 indicates CPU related fault.

3.**Detail error message:-** Brief description of error is display on the screen.

ex: INTR#1 means interrupt controller 1 failed

initial program load (IPL)

An initial program load (IPL) is the act of loading a copy of the operating system from disk into the processor's real storage and executing it.IPL (initial program load) is a mainframe term for the loading of the operating system into the computer's main memory . **Initial Program Load**, **IPL** is the first initial step of loading an operating system on a computer. A mainframe operating system (such as OS/390) contains many megabytes of code that is customized by each installation, requiring some time to load the code into the memory.

Hard disk drive troubleshooting

1.Problem:-

Computer is running slowly or operating programs on hard disk has become slow

Solution:-

•The volume on your hard disk may have excessively fragmented. Analyze and then defragment the volumes on your hard disk if necessary.

2.Problem:-

Hard disk drive not detected

Solution:-

•Miss alignment of power/interface cable or wrong setting of master/slave jumper. Then verify the HDD power/ interface cable and verify master/slave jumper setting.

3.Problem:-

Hard disk drive is not bootable nor accessible at all.

Solution:-

•Wrong configuration and hard disk is dead

•Detect your hard disk in CMOS setup , if it can detect then there may be operating system is crash.

4.Problem:-

The hard disk drive generate more noise

Solution:-

•Run diagnostic on the HDD. Replace drive if diagnostic testing reveals a failure.

•Back up your important data it may be dead soon.

5.Problem:-

“No ROM basic system halted “ error message during startup

Solution:-

•Drive is not install properly so verify that device is install properly.

•There is no active partition so set active partition using FDISK or other utility program.

Preventive Maintenance Tool

Hardware tools:-

1.multimeter/ ohmmeter

2.Oscilloscope

3.Logic analyzer

4.Logic probe

5.Logic pulsar

6.Current tracer

Software tools:-

1.diagnostic software

2.Disk utility software

1.**Multimeter/ Ohmmeter:-**

A multimeter can use for measurement of resistance, voltage, current and also test the continuity of cable.It has low cost and simple working.Used for checking short circuit or open circuit .

2.**Logic analyzer:-**

It is multichannel oscilloscope with memory.Using logic analyzer it is possible to see the entire data bus at one time which can analyze the logic level for each bit on the bus for any time. Logic analyzer can uncover hardware defect that are not found in simulation.

3.**Oscilloscope:-**

An oscilloscope helps to resolve almost any problem in a PC . It is useful in three level of testing.

a)To test logic level

b)To measure various signal characteristics such as pulse width, frequency, rise and fall time, noise etc.

c)To measure relationship between two or more signals.

4.**Logic probe:-**

It is used to find out the logic state of any node in a circuit.There are three color LED on probe:Red and green indicate high and low state respectively An amber LED indicate a pulse.When the logic probe is either connected to an invalid logic level or not connected at all, none of the LEDs light up.

5.**Logic pulsar:-**

The logic pulse is handheld tool used to inject pulses at the input of gate under test.A signal pulse or stream of pulses at different frequencies is issued as per the user's choice.

6.**Current tracer:-**

It is hand held tool which detect current flow in electronic circuit.It is useful in locating shorted components ,track, solder bridge, vcc to ground short ,etc.

Layman check :

Without systematic approach, some problems can be quickly resolved by adopting few shortcuts these are known as layman checks.

Layman check can be applied by not technical person.

Following list provides some important layman checks.

1. Is main AC power is on?
2. Does SMPS switch is on?
3. Is SMPS fan work?
4. Is AC power plug connected?
5. Is CMOS setup parameters correct?
6. Is monitor contrast control in maximum?
7. Is monitor brightness control in maximum?

****

Printed by Libri Plureos GmbH in Hamburg, Germany